Delusive Healers of India

(Phenomenological Approach to Therapy)

Janetius, PhD.

ISBN: 1515229467
ISBN-13: 978-1515229469
Amazon CreateSpace Independent Publishing Platform
United States of America

Dr. S.T. Janetius
Director, Centre for Counselling & Guidance
Sree Saraswathi Thyagaraja College
Pollachi-South India

Delusive Healers
Indigenous Healing and Medicine
Phenomenological Counselling
Traditional Healers of India
Culture-specific Therapy

**Dedicated
to my
Loving Daughter**

Contents

Acknowledgments   i

Chapter 1   Introduction   01

Chapter 2   Worldview   15

Chapter 3   Counselling & Psychotherapy   23

Chapter 4   The Pipe Sapper   33

Chapter 5   The Pulsating Patter   39

Chapter 6   The Medicinal Gagger   47

Chapter 7   Analysis of Healing   55

Chapter 8   Implications for psychotherapy   63

Chapter 9   Phenomenology   71

Chapter 10   Indian Psychology & Counselling   89

References   103

Acknowledgments

The success of this project depends largely on the encouragement and guidelines of many people. Special thanks to my students who have been instrumental in identifying traditional healers for my research. My endless conversations with Dr Mini, Prof. Ravishankar, and Prof. Padmanabhan played a big role in conceptualising the specific indigenous healers as *Delusive Healers*.

I am grateful to my students who are my source of inspiration and proudly remember their constant love and support. I take this opportunity to express my debt of gratitude to Ms. Shilpa who did the final fine-tuning of this book; also my students Jemal Amare and Robel Araya for their timely assistance.

.

One

Introduction

ℳy interest in applying phenomenology to counselling and psychotherapy started very recently. During my doctoral research among the indigenous people in the Cordillera Mountains in the Philippines, while studying their health concepts and healing practices and worldview, I realised that the Western patterns of identifying and classifying mental illness and behavioural problems do not fit well in their life-world. Although many of their sicknesses could be classified as *psychosomatic* from a Western therapeutic perspective, a closer look proved different. Due to the uniqueness of their experiences and worldview, I conceptualised some of their sicknesses as *pneumasomatic* (Janetius, 2003). From then on, my approach to psychology, counselling and psychotherapy took a dramatic turn, from a cross-cultural perspective to culture-specific approach. To this effect, phenomenology came to my rescue. In this book, by studying some unique traditional healers of South India, identifying some of their inimitable concepts, an indigenous counselling model is introduced applying phenomenological concepts.

3

Religion, magic, health and wellbeing are inseparable in any traditional community. For the traditional psyche, it does not matter whether healing is shamanic, faith based, magically attuned, religious, supernatural or scientific. With a simple reasoning of getting a cure, they seek help in their ailments. To say that indigenous ritual healing work due to the power of belief or the placebo effect does not explain fully the underlying process of healing. However, researches done in different traditional communities provide a preliminary scientific explanation for how folk healing methods can affect a patient's illness (Weil, 1995). These findings confirm that our state of mind can influence our response to physical illnesses, especially infectious or inflammatory diseases. As Hultkrantz (1992) points out, many traditional ritual healing practices do work by influencing the mental attitude in the patient.

Due to the strong conventional cultural beliefs influencing the worldview of the people and its relation to health problems, the Western patterns of psychology and therapy modalities need to integrate and assimilate Indian cultural worldview and unique traditional healing modalities. Psychology and psychiatry professionals can enhance their skills by being more open to the therapeutic beliefs and practices of traditional healers (Vontress, 2009). Preparing an indigenous counselling and psychotherapy model by incorporating the existing traditional, cultural components, in view of helping the people more efficiently, would be a real challenge to psychologists and other clinicians in India.

India is a land rooted deep in traditions and religious practices dating back to many centuries. Indian society is also known for numerous conventional healing practices that are often interwoven with religion, culture, magic and bizarre rituals. Traditional healing methods are widely used to treat physical as well as psychological illnesses in India and Western models of counselling and psychotherapy are not very popular among people. Mental health is also one of the most neglected health aspects in rural India in terms of physical facilities as well as trained mental health professionals (Thara & Srinivasan, 2000).

Indian history, heritage and civilization, with exclusive cultural religious practices and literatures, dates back to early Iron Age. Indian civilization is also known for many systematic medical schools like *Ayurveda*, *Siddha* and *Unani,* together with a variety of healing practices that are interwoven with different religious, cultural, magical and shamanic rituals. These healing practices are widely used even today to treat physical as well as psychological illness in India. However, counselling per se has not existed in the Indian subcontinent as a well-defined therapeutic modality.

Although psychology in India is fully interwoven with the ancient philosophical and religious systems, knowledge related to mental health and human behaviour are not clearly articulated or noticeably applied in the daily living. People tend to attribute various mental health issues to evil spirits, evil eye or supernatural powers and prefer to go for magico-religious remedies even these days. The Western models of counselling and psychotherapy are not popular among the majority within the population except at few urban centres. According to a government survey, there is one psychiatrist for every 400,000 people in India (Kennedy, 2010).

In this current Indian scenario, the demands of industrial globalisation and the globalised education that influences various sectors, consequently have introduced counselling and guidance services in a minimal way. However, as acknowledged in many parts around the world, the therapeutic counselling that focuses on the comprehensive development of the person has not become popular, except for some urban centres. Taken as a whole, counselling is narrowly identified and popularly associated with academic advising, career guidance and, further in the industrial setting as performance counselling. Sweeping changes have been seen in the past few decades in the Indian society in the above mentioned areas, however, it is still in the infancy stage.

Traditionally, in the Indian society, there is a strict control over the individual and their actions by caste and creed norms; added to that, elders in the family, family culture (whether the family is joint, nuclear or extended) and the local village governing body also play a vital role in regulating human behaviour. However, this scenario is slowly changing today due to education, mass media, migration to urban centres, massive urbanisation and globalisation.

The emerging Indian society is the outcome of political history India that has undergone at different times and the consequential paradigm shifts one bearing on the other; the change continues. The ancient history of India undoubtedly portrays a sacred, spiritual society which was dominated and guided by philosophical, theological, geographical and political concepts glued together. This social milieu of sacredness and social living underwent a sea of change due to subsequent Muslim invasions, giving way to male dominance and prescribed gender roles, prohibitions in man-woman social contacts, expression of affection, and further confining women behind the veils and the inner walls of the house; added to that, the influence of colonial rulers of Europe who introduced Victorian mores together with the dualistic theology of Judaism and Christianity with a strong eschatological overture created new morals and ethics (Janetius, Mini & Ravishankar, 2009).

The modern day liberated morals depicted through movies, casually lived across the country, impose a new sensual and consumerist social outlook. This sensual concept that has been depicted as a liberated concept is a new attraction to Gen X-ers, Millennials and Gen Z-ers even in the remotest rural communities and the younger generation run berserk falsifying and dethroning many of the Indian traditional cultural norms.

The current Indian society, therefore, appears conservative in the core and liberal in the external. This is further evidenced by the widening gap between the social norms and social behaviour. As the society transforms from a conservative towards liberal, it is viewed by the younger generation as progressive, on the contrary, as deviance by older generation (Janetius, Mini & Ravishankar, 2009). This dichotomous situation is the defining factor of social outlook, socio-cultural living and consequential behavioural pattern seen among people today.

WHO (2005) has estimated that about 5.8% of the total population in India has one or another mental-health problem. A very high rate of suicide is reported in India with a ratio of 17.38 suicides per 100,000 people (Jacob, Sharan, Mirza, Garrido-Cumbrera, Seedat, Mari, Sreenivas & Saxena, 2007). Smoking, drinking and disorders related to mood, emotions and thoughts are also widespread among the population. Figures show 12.2% of men smoke more than 10 cigarettes a day, and 3.2% of men drink alcohol every day (National Family Health Survey 2005). The prevalence of affective disorders was found to be 34 per 1000 population (Ganguli, 2000).

The fascinating issue is that a person with a mental health problem does not believe, accept or understand that s/he has a problem, so also people who live with them, due to lack of awareness and also cultural acceptance of certain behaviours. For example, a person who drinks excessively and abuses his wife at home is not diagnosed as a person with mental health issue rather the situation is apparently seen as two ordinary problems of men in general: a) he drinks excessively and wastes money, b) abuses his wife; or, it could be seen as a single problem: when he drinks, he abuses his wife. The consequences of drinking which results in abuse of wife, poor parenting, troubled socio-emotional living condition, and psycho-social disturbances are often overlooked and ignored. *Therefore, awareness and identification of the mental health problem itself is lacking among people.* Psychosis and severe mental problems like schizophrenia and the like are the ones commonly perceived as mental health problems by many in India today, both the educated as well as illiterate population.

The government of India together with the help of many social work organizations and NGOs have taken various steps to create awareness as well as to educate people about mental health issues. With the implication that removing the stigma attached to mental illness will give social acceptance, community-based health care system has been introduced to bring massive changes at the grassroots levels, by using the members within the communities, to educate people in diagnosing and raising awareness. This supportive system remains to be an effective method of providing primary preventative mental health care (Chatterjee, Chowdhary, Pednekar, Cohen, Andrew, Araya, Simon, 2008). However, the whole concept of mental health in India largely revolves around psychiatry and clinical psychology, giving lesser room for counselling and psychotherapy or other ordinary psychological assistance.

Counselling that has become popular in the West as a distinct therapy modality has not been practiced in the Indian subcontinent, although scholars identify glimpses of Western counselling patterns and similar interventions in the ancient Hindu sacred writings. One of the highly acclaimed citations is in *Bhagavad Gita* where Lord Krishna works out for a change of behaviour through verbal communication with the hesitant Arjuna at the battle field of *Kurukshethra*. One can also see a lot of verbal communicative guidance as normal part of life in India often provided by elders, village heads, priests, and a variety of magical, religious, delusive and fraudulent healers as well. *These barefoot counsellors are popular as well as effective at times.*

Following the empirical, experimental traditions of Wilhelm Wundt, Western psychology was introduced in the first decades of 20th century as a discipline at Calcutta University (Jain, 2005). With the colonial influence and the assorted educational system, British School of Psychology became popular in the academic arena. After the independence, in the 1960's psychologists realised that psychology failed to make an impact in the life of the country and people, especially on the social arena (Sinha, 1994). With the intention of developing research in the area of Humanities and Social Sciences, the Government of India established an autonomous organisation named *Indian Council of Social*

Science Research (ICSSR) in 1968, and researches within the field slowly developed (Jain, 2005). Nevertheless, as seen in the developed countries, psychology has not penetrated the life of the society.

In the recent years, the industrial and educational globalisations have demanded the introduction of counselling and guidance services in India in a broader way. Even so, it is early to say that therapeutic counselling and psychotherapy have received popularity and recognition as in many developed countries. Whilst therapeutic counselling is slowly gaining grounds, reputation and credence, the efficient intervention and effective therapy outcome are tainted by cultural insensitiveness and the blind adherence to Western theories and models of therapy (Soundararajan, 2009). Although some therapists integrate yoga and meditation practices into counselling and psychotherapy process (Clay, 2002), the whole phenomenon is handicapped due to lack of indigenous therapeutic models that take into consideration the culture of the people, define precisely the therapy setting, distinctive counselling process, culture-specific theory bases and exclusive mode of practice which would influence the smooth flow of a therapy process-outcome to satisfy the Indian mind.

As an initiative to prepare indigenous therapy modalities well-suited to the Indian psyche, some unique traditional healing practices are studied. Three specific healers, five people who experienced healing from such healers and seven people who patronise this healing were the subjects in this pilot study. This exploratory-descriptive study employed grounded theory qualitative methodology; in-depth interviews, participant observations and disguise observations were the methods used to collect data. A thorough analysis of their healing modality is explored to draw some postulates to make possible a new form of indigenous therapeutic counselling and culture-specific psychotherapy in particular, indigenous psychology in general for India. While studying the unique healers, the research identified some exclusive characteristics, obvious commonalities and subtle differences. Prompted by the uniqueness of these healers and their popularity among rural communities in this day of scientific developments, categorized the healers as *delusive healers* and their therapy as delusive healing.

Delusive healing is defined in the following way:

"Delusive healing is a therapy modality of some traditional healers who covertly perceive the sickness to be psychosomatic and induce cure using bizarre techniques and practices by deceiving the patients".

Although apparently delusive healing looks like some form of magical or religiomagical healing, there are some major differences noticed. Delusive healers primarily identify the sickness as psychosomatic and then delude the clients by enacting removal of some physical objects from the body to alleviate pain and induce a cure. There are key similarities and subtle differences between the three healers who are studied.

All the three healers have the following commonalities:
- The healers easily identify the sickness as psychosomatic
- Will not reveal to the client or anyone that the sickness is psychosomatic
- The healer expects the client to have tried and failed one or another medical model treatment to confirm that the sickness is psychosomatic in nature
- Ventures into bizarre healing modality, which is basically pretension and delusion, pertinent to the ascribed sickness and convenient to the healer

Exploring delusive healing further, it is acknowledged that the healers show many important characteristics needed for quality counselling as per the Western perspective. More than that, some indigenous methods to create trust, empathy and other basic counselling skills are employed by the healers.

Specific implications that are drawn from the study pave the way for indigenous psychology, therapeutic counselling and culture-specific psychotherapy for Indian psyche.

Studying this complex traditional, cultural healing phenomenon has initiated some indigenous counselling and psychotherapy models, which are far beyond client-centred or transpersonal approach; probably fit within the framework of phenomenological approach. The book also talks about phenomenological counselling and psychotherapy together with a unique indigenous counselling model for the Indian psyche.

Two

Worldview

The word *worldview* has received considerable attention in the past several years. According to Funk (2001) worldview is one's philosophy of life, mindset and outlook on life, formula for life, ideology, faith, or even religion. Worldview affects how a person views different aspects of life - physical, emotional, spiritual, moral, sociological and mental. Thus, worldview is of utmost importance in giving a meaning and purpose to our life and existence. Worldview is rarely questioned or examined because it is a set of preconceived unconscious concepts and a frame of a thought process, and people believe them by default, as a basis for judging the world around them and making choices in life. Worldview is very dynamic; it is neither fixed reality nor completely expressed. Throughout history, the worldview has been constantly updated whenever personal experience and discovery happened. Subsuming the preceding worldviews, new worldviews emerge (Leith, 2003). Education, religion and openness to another culture are some of the influential factors that facilitate the process of new worldviews, and it is a perennial process (Janetius, 2003).

The World Health Organisation (1976) defines a healer as someone who is recognised by the community as an experienced person to offer health care services, using various methods based on the social, cultural and religious belief systems. Almost in all traditional societies there is a belief that disease is caused by natural or supernatural causes. It is due to this reason, from time memorial, treatments used to be a mixture of religion and local culture. Charms and talismans were commonly used in all cultures. Traditional healing practices that are common among indigenous communities definitely reflect their worldview.

In African cultures, people believe that sickness can be caused by witchcraft and health is restored by maintaining harmony with other people, spirits and ancestors such as recently departed family members. Orthodox Christian Ethiopians believe that certain sickness can be cured by fasting and holy water (Janetius, Mini, & Alemayehu, 2010). In some Nigerian communities, people believe that interpersonal clashes can cause sickness, and native healers encourage confession as a remedy (Offiong, 1999).

The Indian philosophical system identifies human body made up of five elements seen throughout the universe, i.e., water, fire, earth, wind, and ether and traditional *Ayurveda* healing practice advocates homeostasis between the elements of the universe in the body in order to obtain a remedy for any sickness (Ramakrishna & Weisss, 1992). Filipinos believe that sorcery can be used to inflict illness and therefore, look for religio-magical remedies (Edman & Kameoka, 1997).

Today psychologists have become aware of the importance of considering a client's cultural background when assessing the problem and determining treatment. Techniques that might be effective in the West or similar cultures might be inappropriate for a client from Eastern countries. Therefore, there is a call among psychologists to situate subjective experiences of human beings and behaviour. In order to understand human conditions of clients for effective therapy, therapists must be aware of their own cultural biases and adopt a cultural outlook.

The ancient time-tested traditional approach to healing is seen as a holistic approach in contrast to the Western medical models that focus solely on the physical aspect of healing (Benor, 1999). It is a common belief among people, especially in the traditional communities that illnesses are some sort of war waged by spiritual powers, be it a witch, sorcerer, a spirit, ancestor or demon, possibly seeking retribution for acts of commission or omission. Because of this worldview, people expect healing to be brought about, not merely by technical, clinical procedures or chemical concoctions but with some magical remedies in tune with their belief system. Therefore, the worldview plays a vital role in understanding health concepts and healing practices.

Psychotherapy and counselling approaches do go beyond the popular Western medical models to some extent. However, the diversity of cultural differences is often neglected due to resistance of many Euro-Western scholars and their lack of openness to specific ethno-cultural groups and ideologies. Some Western psychologists even argue that the study of culture and ethnicity belongs to the fields of anthropology (Trimble, 2000). Focusing on certain particulars like tradition, culture, worldview, belief-system and specific community behaviour patterns will help mental health professionals in identifying and solving many specific mental health issues. Understanding the specific attitudes toward health, illness, psychological distress, and healing modalities of different cultures will enable the counsellor to conduct counselling and psychotherapy in the lives and thoughts of countless ethno-cultural groups, which are ignored in the main body of psychology. So there is a need today to study the traditional cultural practices and worldview so that psychotherapy becomes applicable and useful to all cultures and peoples.

In India, developing an indigenous psychology and psychotherapy has been the focal point of discussion for the past few decades (Sinha, 1993, 2000). Although many steps have been taken in the last decade to identify Indian psychology in order to formulate appropriate indigenous therapy models, the imitative still remains at the beginning stage (Adair, Puhan, & Vohra, 1993). This suggests that the traditional native healing patterns in the Indian subcontinent have not been fully explored and integrated into psychotherapeutic processes due to lack of interest and research in this area. Identifying the worldview, belief systems and health practices of the clients would therefore enable therapists to be more effective in dealing with clients who come from varying culture and belief systems.

Three

Counselling &
Psychotherapy

$\mathcal{H}$istory of medicine started with a fusion of facts, folklore, and superstitions. Counselling and psychotherapy evolved from ministrations of priests, shamans, magicians, soothsayers and witch doctors of the ancient world. Understanding the human condition subjectively, these traditional healers attempted to determine the causes of both physical and emotional distress.

Krippner (1988) explains that behaviour therapy, hypnotherapy, psychodrama, NLP, etc., are closely parallel to the traditional native healing methods. Contemporary psychotherapy that took a new shape from Sigmund Freud and his concept *religion is infantile neurosis* paved way to rule out many subjective experiences. Besides this, under the pretext of being very scientific in its approach, contemporary psychology has compartmentalised human condition and evaded subjective spiritual, religious or faith experiences that are inscribed in the minds of many people.

Today psychologists have become aware of the importance of taking a client's cultural background into account when assessing the problem and determining treatment. Scholars recognize that most therapies are based on Western systems of psychology, which stress the desirability of individualism and independence. However, cultures of Asia emphasize different values, such as conformity, dependency on others, and obeying one's parents, etc. Techniques that might be effective in the West or similar cultures might be inappropriate for a client from India. Therefore there is a call among psychologists to be culture-specific and culturally competent to situate subjective experiences of human beings and behaviour. As Frie (2003) points out,

"with the advent of post-modernism, the unity of the individual mind, the notion of an objectivity, knowable world, and the view of language as the carrier of truth have all been implicitly or explicitly rejected...(in contrast) postmodernism asserts that the person, or subject, is not only shaped, but also subverted by the contexts in which it exists" (p.2).

In order to understand human conditions of clients for effective therapy outcome, therapists must be aware of their own cultural biases and adopt a phenomenological outlook.

It's hard to differentiate counselling and psychotherapy. Counselling psychology that became popular after World War II served relatively healthy clients who experience difficulties related to interpersonal relationships, adjustment difficulties, life crises and stresses. On the other hand, psychotherapy dealt with severely disturbed individuals. Today, this distinction between psychotherapy and counselling is quite vague and both terms are often used interchangeably. Counsellors and psychotherapists often treat the same kinds of problems with the same sets of techniques. However, a slim difference that can still be made between counselling and psychotherapy would be: counselling is less intensive and more focused toward listening, direction setting, and issues that don't require in-depth analysis where as psychotherapy is more on dealing with emotional problems, neurosis, and more of therapy focused.

In the Indian context, many a time, advice and similar help offered by pastors, community leaders and social workers who have a little or no training at all in specific fields of counselling or guidance or therapy often claim their informal help or advice as counselling and therapy. Counselling and Psychotherapy differs from such bare-foot pseudo-counsellors.

- First and foremost, counselling or psychotherapy is not about advice giving.

- Secondly, counselling and psychotherapy in their truest sense are establishing working relationships by a trained, qualified clinician in which treatment methods and techniques are guided by a well-developed theoretical framework. The client comes with a presenting problem; the therapist and patient establish a working relationship; the therapist defines the problem, and once it is defined, suggests solution.

Acceptance or approval for psychology, counselling and psychotherapy is wanting in India. Mental illness and psychological disturbance of a person are not considered common human illness, and so there is stigma attached to people who seek counselling and psychotherapy. Even people who seek therapy and counselling are often afraid to talk in public about their therapy because of social backlash.

Western and developed countries are far advanced in accepting psychotherapy and counselling as much-needed fields of science and medicine that such stigma seen in Indian culture associated with people seeking counselling and psychotherapy are not seen there. It is, however, true to say that even in the Asian societies such discrimination and stigma have decreased significantly. Seeking therapeutic assistance for emotional and similar problems is slowly becoming a common phenomenon even in India and other Eastern societies.

Over the last few decades the field of counselling and psychotherapy expanded enormously in the number of approaches, the numbers of people enter the profession and the numbers of clients opt for therapeutic assistance.

Before 1950, psychoanalysis, the therapy module started by Sigmund Freud that focused on the unconscious, early-childhood experiences and the inner world of the client were virtually the only form of psychotherapy. In the later years, many theorists have developed many other psychodynamic therapies, some even significantly different from Freud's original techniques. In the 1950s and 1960s, behavioural therapies that focus more on the learning, stimulus-response interactions emerged as a second force. In the next few years, humanistic-existential therapies known otherwise phenomenological therapies came as third force in psychology; client-centred and transpersonal approaches have become popular over the course of time. As the number of approaches to therapy grew, the practice of psychotherapy and counselling spread from clinical to non-clinical settings, which was conducive to its becoming popular all over the world today. In India, although counselling has not penetrated schools, industries and similar areas, the future is very encouraging.

Both in counselling and psychotherapy, treatment of individuals with emotional and behavioural problems are primarily done through verbal communications, although there is a move in America to introduce some kind of pharmacy training to psychotherapists. In most types of therapy, a person discusses his or her problems one-on-one basis with a therapist. The therapist tries to understand the person's problems and to help change the distressing thoughts, feelings, or behaviours. Besides such individual therapy, group therapy or group session is also a common therapeutic modality, where a therapist or a group of therapists facilitates a group of people.

Today there are more than 250 kinds of therapy, but only a fraction of these have found mainstream acceptance. Most dominant therapeutic approaches could be classified as (1) psychodynamic, (2) behavioural, (3) cognitive, (4) existential-humanistic, and (5) eclectic.

Psychodynamic approaches focus on the anxiety provoking situations, unconscious mechanisms and early-childhood experiences to identify cliental problems. Dream analysis and free association of clients' thoughts are some of the traditional techniques.

As against the concept of Freudian unconscious, behavioural approaches focus on the observable and measurable behaviours. All our behaviours are learned so we can unlearn; based upon this principle, the behaviourists help individuals to replace the distressing behaviours with more appropriate ones.

Cognitive approaches emphasize the beliefs and thoughts. Irrational beliefs or distorted thinking patterns can cause a variety of problems that lead to mental and behavioural problems and the therapists direct people to think more rational, constructive ways.

Humanistic-existential approaches focus on the client's present life situation, aspirations and motivations in understanding, shaping and modifying behaviour. Therapists show empathy and care to facilitate clients toward personal realizations and decision-making, take responsibility for their actions, to accept themselves, and to recognize their own potential for growth and change. Eclectic therapy is an integrative approach of one or more theories and therapies put together. Today many therapists prefer this approach.

Four

The Pipe Sapper

The common understanding among people that undigested food can cause pain in the stomach is the underlying theory of this delusive healer's curative action. Only those who experience pain in the abdomen, or people with discomfort from the thought that some food stuff or related substance is stagnant in the stomach, come to this healer for therapy.

It was a fine morning and the number of people waiting to see the healer was around twelve that include both the patients and accompanying persons. People were standing and squatting under a tree in front of the healer's house. It was around 9.30 in the morning and there was a small rush to move to the portico of the house as the healer came out of his house with his assistant.

The healer was a 54 year-old married male; belonged to Hindu religion residing in a rural village of Tamil Nadu and speaks Tamil language. His family is doing this traditional healing for three generations now.

The healer is a simple, peasant-like person and his way of talking revealed that he is unschooled. He is very courteous, gracious and has a big smiling face. He has dressed neatly, using a white dhoti (popular loin cloth) and a white cotton shirt with a white towel on his left shoulder. He sits casually in a steel folding chair and requests graciously the patient to come forward.

The patient is a 44 year old male, accompanied by his wife. The patient moves forward towards the healer and the healer's assistant seats him on a chair. The healer nods his head to signal the patient to narrate his story.

The patient slowly starts to narrate his ailment and his wife interrupts. The healer politely forbids her and encourages the man to speak. He then unwearyingly listens to the patient as he reports his sickness, pain and dilemma.

The healer devotedly asks the client to recall in retrospect, all the details of food eaten in the last few days, recollecting the events starting back to the origin of pain in the stomach. The healer also gets the details of treatments undergone in the hospitals with modern medicine. He also enquires about the family details, whether there were quarrels between husband and wife, misunderstanding among in-laws, neighbours, etc. The healer further clarifies with the patient, whether he could suspect any reason for the pain. As it is customary among the people to come to this healer with a belief that there is stagnated undigested food stuff in the stomach, the patient calmly suggests that he ate some meat few days ago in one of his in-law's house, and that was the starting of the stomach pain.

Without countering the narrations and the proposed cause recollected by the patient, the healer politely concurs with the patient with a keen eye contact. And without any hesitation, the healer agrees and speculates openly that it may be a bone piece or curry-leave that is left in the stomach could cause the pain.

After clarifying few more details of the nature of pain and the previous medicines/treatments he took in the hospital, the healer gets ready to begin his therapy session.

The therapy session is very simple, and the technique used by the healer is out of the ordinary. He asks his assistant (a pale thin fellow who stands beside him) to bring water, and he gives it to the patient in a big jug full, to drink. Once the patient drank his stomach full, the healer takes a small piece of pipe specially designed for his healing purpose, inserts it into the mouth of the patient with the help from his assistant and pushes down slowly into the stomach. The face of the patient shows that he senses the pipe entering the throat and down, as if there is some mild pain. The healer ceremoniously takes the other end of the pipe into his own mouth and blows the air slowly and steadily into the stomach of the patient. With a small body niggle the patient slightly moves as the air bubbles waggle inside the stomach. The assistant carefully holds the patient with a stare (rebuking him for moving his body). The healer then slowly sucks the pipe with the motive to search for something inside the stomach of the patient. After few minutes of laparoscopic search, the healer shows signs of enthusiasm and takes the pipe out of his mouth and shows the patient a small piece of bone. The face of the patient now glees and signs of hope emerge as he sees with his own eyes some stagnant bone piece is taken from the stomach.

The patient gets up from the chair; he and his wife move politely to pay some payment to the healer. There is no prescribed payment; 50 to 100 Rupees is the expected minimum payment which goes up to 500 rupees, if the patient is wealthy. Once the assistant has collected the payment, the healer is getting ready to meet his next client.

Five

The Pulsating Patter

ℙulsating Patter is a 54 year old Hindu male from a small village in Chittor taluk of in Kerala State, specialised in healing wounds that are not cured for a longer period. He is an uneducated person, going for daily wages in the farmlands and speaks Malayalam and a little Tamil. He is married and has two sons; both are minimally educated, married and employed. People call him *thanthri* (a misguiding name because this word is used in Kerala to address respectfully a temple priest of great eminence; however, to call the healer as *thantri* would mean only – a man of techniques or tricks). He started his healing at the age of 20 after seeing a healer doing this healing. He framed his own therapy modality with a self-formulated mixture of magico-religious bizarre practices. The healer is also known for doing magico-religious healing for witchcraft. As he narrates,

"I have the divining power to differentiate wounds caused by witchcraft, evil spirits or evil-eye and, sickness caused by foreign objects like a thorn or nails. It is the secret of my therapy and success of my therapy".

He has no special place or clinic for healing. Since he is practicing in a part-time basis, he usually goes to the house of the sick people and does the therapy sessions there. If at all, someone comes to his home for therapy, he entertains them, then and there.

The healer has some specific rituals before doing any therapy session. The preparation for therapy is drinking a bottle of brandy or whisky (quarter -180ml) which the healer demands from the family members of the patients or whoever comes to invite him for therapy. He does not drink local liquors like toddy or arrack, which are cheaply available. An old lady justified, *"he does not drink for the sake of intoxication before the therapy sessions but rather due to the particular technique he employs, which needs physical contact with the ulcers and wounds, and it is very aversive"*.

After drinking the alcohol, he comes to the house of the client, or he drinks in the house of the clients before starting therapy sessions.

He first listens benevolently to the patients and after listening blissfully, gives a methodical inspection of the wound as if checking whether it is physical wound or something caused by witchcraft. If he decides that he can deal with the case with his unique delusive healing, he tells the patient that the wound is caused by some foreign particles staying inside the body. If he decides otherwise, he prescribes magico-religious healing at his home. For delusive healing, he does not demand any money except a small bottle of brandy before the treatment and, after the session is over, expects the clients to pay some money as gift; generally people pay a minimum of 200 rupees.

The following is a description of a healing ceremony conducted at the house of a patient where the healer was invited.

The patient was a 30 year old married lady with two children. She and her husband work in the paddy fields and live in a rural village. She had a wound in the left leg near the thumb which she got it while working in the paddy fields few months ago. She is not aware what exactly caused the wound to appear. She only suspects that it is from the field that she got it. Since the wound was small, she did not attend any medicine in the beginning.

As days passed by, the wound did not cure, and she went to a small clinic near her house and paid more than 300 rupees for cleaning and applying medicines. Though there were signs of cure in the beginning, it did not heal fully, and she had difficulties going to job at times. At this juncture, her mother suggested getting the assistance of the healer whom her mother knows.

The healer was brought in a motorcycle by the husband of the patient. When the healer entered the house, the alcohol was given to him to drink. The mother of the lady who was standing beside whispered in my ears that the method used by the healer is very aversive one, and he needs to drink to do that.

The healer asked the patient to sit on a chair and went on checking the leg of the lady squatting on the ground in front of her. He unwearyingly listened to her story of the ailment. After listening for few minutes and having a closer look at the wound, confirmed that there is some foreign object still in the body, and it has to be removed.

He, then lighted a camphor in the middle of the house and recited some prayers in Malayalam language, which is very hard to comprehend. After few minutes of prayers, he started to stroke the leg of the patient from knee and downwards, muttering the prayers. This kind of tapping and stroking went on for around 15 minutes. Slowly, he changed from tapping to massage downward as if trying to push something from the upper part of the leg towards downward.

Once this was also done for few minutes, the healer drank some alcohol and bent down a little bit and licked the wound of the lady with his tongue, and showed from his mouth a small piece of a stick which he claimed taken from the wound.

The lady who was suffering and the family people gave a sigh of relief, and the healer felt jubilant. The healer stood up with an understanding that the healing ceremony is over. He requested the husband of the lady to get some herbal paste from his house when he drops him at home and asked the lady to apply it on the wound. The wound was healed within two weeks time.

Six

The Medicinal Gagger

There is a wide-spread belief among educated as well as uneducated rural and urban population that certain medicines, chemical combinations or herbal concoctions could be given to people without the knowledge of the person who consumes, through food, to disturb the wellbeing of a person or entice a person secretly towards the whims and fancy of another person. With this belief system, when people feel psychologically disturbed by a recurring thought of a person or place which they don't like or depressed or physically and mentally weak by some unknown feelings, do believe they are being allured by someone through food. The part of the belief also holds that this particular enticing poisonous food stuff that went to the stomach will not digest and remains in the stomach causing sickness or uneasiness and disturbance as long as it remains inside. Here, this healing practice becomes a rescue.

This is the story of a 67 year old male teacher, who runs a private tuition centre for students. The client was experiencing psychological distress, sleeplessness and also recurring thoughts of a lady who was dismissed by him from the office recently. The lady was working at his office for more than a year and was managing almost all the activities at the centre when he was present as well as absent. The client would be in the centre only three days in a week as he was working as a part-time teacher in a college; he really needed a trustworthy person to look after his tuition centre and was happy that the particular lady was taking care of the centre.

It so happened one day when questioned about her negligence of duty, the lady got angry at the client. The client felt that he lost his self-esteem by her answering back rudely and decided to terminate her. The next day morning when she came for the job, he politely requested her not to come for the job anymore. The client did not feel guilt for dismissing her because she also had the habit of frequently quarrelling with another officemate. Although the client felt relieved when he dismissed her from the job, a couple of days later felt some uneasiness of unknown nature.

He slowly developed unusual sleep patterns, troubled night sleep and started to have nightmares. The recurring thoughts of the lady also begin to bother him. Whenever he walks inside the office the thought of the lady would flash his mind as if she is present there. He acknowledged that he never had any physical or sexual attraction towards her, although he felt at times that the lady was looking and dealing with him differently. He also confessed that he had no guilt feeling in dismissing her from the job. He went to a nearby clinic, and the doctor checked his blood, sugar level, cholesterol levels and found everything in normal condition. He prescribed him some sleeping tablets that gave him some temporary sleep but his major problem was not solved.

The client recalled a minor incident that happened few months back, which made him think over and over again. The disturbing thought is that she might have given some kind of *kaivisham* (medicine to entice him) through food.

In his own words,

> She was eating rice cake in the office for breakfast. I happen to pass that side, and out of courtesy, she invited me to share the food. I politely refused her offer saying that I had my breakfast few minutes ago and not hungry. However out of consideration, I took a small piece of rice cake from her plate. The next day she bought a separate pack of rice-cake for me and gave me a couple of days. After giving the food she started to show a different kind of attention towards me. As I am not interested in her personally, I did not bother much.

> Now that I have this kind of sleeplessness and the related problems, I do feel strongly that she might have given some strange stuff in the food. I went to the nearby clinic and consulted the doctor, who is a good friend of mine, but didn't to mention anything about this incident to him because this did not come to my mind. Since I am in my sixties the doctor suspected sugar, cholesterol or blood

pressure as the cause and did a through check-up. He was not able to identify anything wrong in my physique. The only medicine he could prescribe was sleeping pills. It worked a bit, but my basic complaints remained.

At this juncture, the thought of eating rice cake came to my mind, and I mentioned this to one of my very close friends. He recommended me to a traditional physician. This traditional healer is basically an herbalist. Primarily I went to the herbalist (locally called *Vaidiyar*) for ordinary medicines only, but I openly narrated him the incidents related to the rice cake and my strong suspicion about enticing chemicals and related stuff often given by people. He agreed with me and gave me an appointment for another day to have a stomach cleaning therapy. He also advised me to come to the clinic in empty stomach.

The stomach cleaning session was arranged on a Saturday afternoon in the backside of his clinic, and the *Vaidiyar* gave me some instructions before starting the therapy session. He told me that the medicine would be a strong one and by the reaction to the medicine, all the stagnated food or chemicals would come out, and I will be relived of my difficulties.

First, he gave me three or four pieces of dried medicinal barks together with some herbal leaves to chew and swallow it. As per his instructions, I chew it and swallowed them although it was extremely bitter. He then asked his assistant to give me water to drink. I presumed that there must be some medicines in the water too, as it was slightly salty. I waited for 20 to 30 minutes and was talking with the herbalist. As he suggested in the beginning after half an hour, I felt uneasiness and start to sweat exceptionally. Slowly, I started to have the sensation of vomiting. Within few minutes, I started to vomit. The *Vaidiyar* showed me a place beneath the tree to throw out. Dark-green coloured paste like dirt came out, and my mouth had a very bitter taste. I washed my mouth and sat down. After few minutes once again I vomited and this time, there was only water no other substance.

The *Vaidiyar* had a close look at the vomited jell like sticky substance, stirring with a long stick which he instantaneously took from a nearby bush. All clear... exclaimed the *Vaidiyar*, and I felt a sense of relief. The *Vaidiyar* came and sat beside me and asked his assistant to bring me a cup of tea. He once again started to ask questions about the food the lady gave me and narrated stories of some other people who came to him for similar problems. As customary I paid him 500 rupees and came back to my house. That night, I had a very peaceful sleep. The disturbing thoughts never came to my mind anymore.

Seven

Analysis of Healing

𝕿he ancient time-tested traditional approach to healing is seen as a holistic approach in contrast to the Western medical models that focus solely on the physical aspect of healing (Benor, 1999). For the traditional psyche, illnesses are some sort of war waged by supernatural powers and because of this traditional worldview people expect healing to be brought about, not merely by technical, clinical procedures or chemical concoctions but with the help of religiomagical remedies in tune with their life-world. The understanding of worldview is very important in comprehending health concepts and healing practices. Since the traditional healers work completely in-tune with the life-world of the people and community in which they live, highly successful. Understanding and exploring the traditional healers will give enormous insights for meaningful understanding of clients in counselling and psychotherapy.

The first healer, *the Pipe Sapper*, convinces the client that he took something from the stomach by a piece of pipe. The second healer *the Pulsating Patter* strikes the veins and the body to draw some foreign stray objects to the face of the wound and then take it through his mouth filled with alcohol. The third healer, *the Medicinal Gagger* gives some colouring herbal barks to eat first and then by chemicals induce the client to vomit and thus shows that some stagnant stuff has been removed from the stomach. All these are done by the healers to convince the clients, who believe that something that entered into the body is the cause of sickness. The healer claims that the foreign objects are taken from the body, and therefore, the clients are unconsciously prepared for a cure.

The first healer is purely a delusive healer; the second one is both delusive as well as religiomagical healer, and the third one is primarily an herbalist involved in delusive healing. The decision to delude and heal comes from the basic identification of the healers that the sickness is psychosomatic.

In the case of the first healer, his healing technique goes in tune with the popular belief that some food stuff (like bones, charcoal, etc...) can be stagnant in the stomach and can cause sickness. The healer identifies himself with the thoughts of the client, although he knows that it is not true. The delusive healer strongly believes that the sickness is caused by the belief of the patient himself that some foreign objects or stagnant food stuff is in the stomach. The healer enacts a ritual in which he deludes the client by showing a charcoal piece or bone piece, as if it is taken from the stomach, which the healer originally hides in the pipe or his mouth.

In the case of the second healer, the very same philosophy is behind the healing ceremony except the nature of sickness is different and the healing modality in which the healer tries to enact the removal differs. The speciality of this second healer is, healing the incurable wounds in the body. It is a common practice among people to walk barefoot and there are ample chances of getting a wound by thorns, stray nails, sharp stones and many other similar objects. Sometimes, sharp objects do stay under the skin and cause ulcers of many kinds. Generally when people get a wound, they do some homemade remedies, and if it does not cure, thinking of going to hospitals. Even after going to hospitals, if the wound is not cured, rural people generally think that some poisonous thorn or some sharp objects might have stayed under the skin and cause the incurable wound, which the medical doctor is not able to identify and cure. In extreme cases, the people even think that the sickness is the effect of witchcraft and evil spirits and therefore, the wound is not cured even after medicines are taken from doctor. In such situations, these traditional healers come to the rescue of the people. The use of alcohol and licking and searching the wound also plays a curative role in the chronic sickness. The healer in the disguise of searching for foreign objects in the wound and removal, first patting above and around the wound area increases the blood circulation. The delusive healer then cleanses the wound with alcohol, which in fact, he drinks and also keeps in the mouth (in disguise) and the herbal medicine that he asks to apply after his healing session induces the healing. However, he deludes the clients and makes them believe that some foreign objects or particles are removed from the body and thus try to cure in tune with the belief system of the client.

In the case of the third healer, the herbal barks given to the client become a thick coloured substance in the stomach and later vomiting it out provides an impression that some stagnated stuff from the body is taken out of the stomach. Seeing this, the clients are made to believe that they are relieved of the poisonous material. This deception of the healer facilitates the patient's chances for a cure. It is therefore, the combination of belief the client has, regarding the cause of the sickness, and the healer's trick in showing the client some elements in tune with the same belief system activates a fast cure in the client.

All the delusive healers clearly perceive the cliental problem as psychosomatic in nature, and the way they deal with the client is simply superb. For example, all the delusive healers empathize with the clients in different ways and means that gives the impression that they are concerned about the wellbeing of the client. This belief is further strengthened by the fact that they don't have any fixed money as a fee. They also give another notion to the clients that healing is the work of God, and no fee should be assigned to that. The healer is ready to come to the house of the clients and show their concern and care. This feeling of one with them is very important for the process of healing. They spend more time with the clients and not bound by short appointment times and other distracting concerns. Active listening is yet another important process of these traditional healers. While listening, they do not contradict, do not impose their values and encourage the clients to narrate their problems, the cause of sickness as they think and understand as well as the cure for their sicknesses. Major therapeutic characteristics identified in Delusive Healers:

- Active listening
- Healer & healee share similar worldview and belief system
- High in empathy
- Non imposition of personal values on the client
- Non-confrontational approach
- Personal attributes of the healer (acceptance of healer as a specialist)
- Ready to serve in the house of the client, if needed
- Spend more time with the clients and create a sense of trust
- Unconditional acceptance of the client

Although deluding the clients would stand equalling to cheating, the main intention of the healer is the cure. This is where they differ from quacks. The lack of transparency in disclosing the nature of the problem to the client is a major negative mark as we look from an ethical point of view, however, the intention is to do something (in whatever possible way) to the benefit of the misfortunate person who suffers. Do the healers confirm with the belief system of the client just as a means of survival and earning money or with the pure intention of cure and the act is morally and ethically acceptable is not the scope of this study. The study is only focused on how the healing is done, what are the underlying concepts and beliefs.

Eight

Implications for Psychotherapy

The concept of Cultural Intelligence (CQ) is gaining momentum today. Cultural Intelligence is the competence of an individual to comprehend, recount, exert efficiently and transversely among cultures. CQ can fetch success in business ventures, managerial positions and leadership arenas, brandishing top-notch distinct personality. Similarly, there is an increasing interest in the role of customs and cultural traditions and in healthcare disciplines because they influence human behaviours and health seeking behaviour. DSM-IV implies that all clinicians should be able to explain cliental problems culturally. It enjoins therapists to be flexible in their therapeutic approaches. Studies have consistently demonstrated that one's culture and worldview are determinants of therapy. Therefore, a competent therapist should learn the different cultural concepts, ethnic identities, and develop specific approaches in order to develop a set of techniques that is consonant with the cultural belief system of their patients.

One important factor the study identifies in the delusive healing is that the patient believes in the power of the treatment and both the healer and healee work in the same set of worldview and mind frame that also can effect a cure.

From the above facts, the research implies that culture, more specifically the client's worldview, and the healer working in tune with the client's belief plays a vital role in the process of healing which need to be considered in therapeutic interventions. From the study of the three healers and their healing modality, the following postulates can be drawn for indigenous counselling and psychotherapy in India.

1. Counsellors and psychotherapists should be flexible enough to facilitate culture-specific approaches in order to reduce the gap between the therapists and the clients.

2. To be a "culturally sensitive therapist" or "culturally relevant therapist" it is mandatory to have a 'client-centred' approach rather than a 'disease-centred' approach which is purely Western module that primarily focuses on the observable symptoms in making a diagnosis, whereas in client-centred therapy how the client defines the problems, the language and terms that are used to express the problems, and what the client believes to be the cause of the problems are taken into consideration.

3. Even though some of the findings of this study, when examined critically could be categorized as fraudulent bizarre behaviours or disappearing folklores, they are

still considered by the people of the land, specifically in the rural communities as an effective means of therapy. In view of this, counsellors and psychotherapists who work for the benefit of the rural populace should utilize one or other cultural therapy modalities as alternative or complementary therapies.

4. During the assessment process, the practitioner must be open and sensitive to the client's worldview, cultural belief systems and how they view their problems. In view of understanding the clients' worldview, the therapist can also look into specific questions like: How does the client define problems? How is health defined? What are the client's beliefs about the cause of the problems? How does the client describe the symptoms? Where does the client go for healing? Where does the client's family traditionally go for healing?

5. Certain therapy settings should be taken into consideration to make the therapy process culturally appropriate. For example, fixed fee structure, artificial settings of healing against helping the client in the house, may be considered inappropriate during therapy by some cultures due to the belief that therapy is an act of divine intervention. Listening actively without questioning the validity of the belief system of the client.

Today the West is moving towards a greater appreciation of nature and the spiritual world and a good example of this is in the field of psychology, due to mainly the efforts of Carl

Jung, Abraham Maslow, Stanislav Grof, Jane Roberts, Charles Tart, Ken Wilber and many others. Psychology that evolved purely as a scientific endeavour in 1879 by Wilhelm Wundt and latter strengthened by behaviourists J. B. Watson, B. F. Skinner, etc., is losing its influence today because of the emergence of cultural psychology and its application in therapeutic settings. In culture-specific psychotherapy, the therapist recognizes the cultural practices, belief system and health concepts behind the client's illness and healing.

As modern cultures and technologies spread around the world, the traditional cultural practices diminish continually as older generations pass away and younger generations slowly set aside their traditional ways and adapt to new life styles. However, the psyche still holds on the remnants of the past and, traditions. Sometimes it can create or lead to inner conflicts too. Therefore many researchers are now placing a greater emphasis on recording indigenous cultures and knowledge. Organizations are being formed to preserve and foster traditional cultures, language and knowledge of various groups of peoples.

In this study, a unique traditional healing style was explored studying three healers and many other people who have close knowledge about such a cultural phenomenon. The findings open a new chapter in understanding and classifying a new kind of healers as *delusive healers'* often ignored or vaguely observed, otherwise generically labelled. Since there are no previous studies done exploring these rural healers from the perspective of cultural-psychology, this study paves the way for integrating traditional belief systems into mainstream psychology and culture-specific psychotherapy. In a day of Western dominance in doctrines, theories and frameworks on mental health and therapeutic interventions, the findings of the study stimulate discussion and create increased understanding of traditional knowledge from local culture and traditional healing practices. By taking a closer look at the therapy process of the delusive healers, one can infer that many counselling processes proposed by the eminent psychologists around the globe need to be adopted in an apt way, acceptable and comprehensible to the local population, so that culture-specific therapy models can emerge. This study gives counsellors and psychotherapists a new perspective in understanding and helping patients coming from rural cultural backgrounds. The study is meaningful for counselling and psychotherapy because it draws postulates for practical consideration to enhance culture-specific therapy.

Nine

Phenomenology

℘henomenology is a philosophical perspective as well as an approach in qualitative research. Husserl understands phenomenology as a discipline that attempts to describe what is given to us in experience, without any obscuring preconceptions or hypothetical speculations (Husserl, 1970). According to Spiegelberg (1970) phenomenology is, "...the direct investigation and description of phenomena as consciously experienced, without theories about their causal explanation and as free as possible from unexamined preconceptions and presuppositions" (p. 810).

The above two simple definitions make it clear that instead of making intellectual speculations about reality, phenomenology advocates to a pure description of *what is*. In short, phenomenology turns away from *a-priori* assumptions and theory to describe the subjective experiences without hypothesizing or imposing itself onto another's understanding. Phenomenology seeks to arrive at the essence of the *noema*[1]. Through descriptive language,

---

[1] Edmund Husserl used noema as a technical term in phenomenology to stand for the object or content of a thought, judgment, or perception.

phenomenology identifies phenomena how the subjects perceive them in a given situation. It is a powerful tool for understanding subjective experiences, gaining insights into people's motivations and actions, and looking through culture-specific assumptions and indigenous wisdom. Free from hypotheses or preconceptions, phenomenological research seeks essentially to describe rather than explain (Husserl, 1970). To this effect, a wide variety of methods are used in phenomenological approach that includes interviews, conversations, participant observation, action research, focus meetings and analysis of personal texts; in short, minimum structure and maximum depth without any theoretical and researcher bias (Gorden, 1969; Oakley, 1981 & Plummer, 1983; Measor, 1985).

Phenomenology was relatively not known outside the philosophical settings before the advent of postmodern thinking. In the last few decades, its implications to psychology and other social sciences have been slowly realised (Kearney, 1984). The three European psychiatrists, Jaspers, Boss and Binswanger, were the first to apply the work of Husserl and Heidegger to make an existential approach to therapy and psychopathology (Mills, 1999).

Today there is a tendency among many psychologists to reduce the inter-human situation to mere scientific scores; furthermore, commit a mistake of treating a theory as a metaphysical assertion. This way of wrong classification of relative or approximate knowledge as absolute knowledge prevents the possibility of getting real meaning of human experience. Conventional psychology seeks to experimentally quantify human relations and try to be objective, thus ignores the subjective understanding and experiencing. This distinction between objective and subjective vanishes in phenomenological questioning where the emphasis is on the subjective nature of all experiences.

Phenomenological approach is more appropriate for counselling and psychotherapy not only because phenomenology is about searching, describing human experiences as it appears but also it studies life-world of people as it appears and as people experience. Belief-systems, that is, the belief of faith and the worldview that a person and the community hold as the innermost cultural, spiritual, psychological resources for healing, are important factors for counselling psychotherapy process (Richards & Bergin, 1997). The effectiveness of therapy depends to a large extent on the quality of the relationship between the client and therapist; better the rapport between therapist and client, better the therapy outcome. This trust or rapport is possible only when a therapist has the openness to conceptualise cliental experiences.

It is a known fact that the various schools of counselling and therapy originate from specific worldviews and theoretical frameworks. How a professional therapist classifies clients' presenting problems are found in DSM[2] and such causes and cures are the creations of Western stereotypes and worldview. It is true that the diagnostic manual of mental disorders (DSM V) that is widely used as a standardised tool of classification of mental sickness encourages clinicians to be culturally sensitive in their therapeutic approaches. However, the classifications in DSM itself are cross-cultural. In contrast, native healers, shamans and other indigenous therapists cling on to the belief system and life-world in healing process, and such a practice is appealing to millions even today (Janetius, 2003).

In counselling and psychotherapy, culture is understood to pose a barrier to quality therapy (Santos, 1998). Psychologists are slowly becoming aware of the fact that people from different ethno-cultural groups do indeed have unique thinking, behaviour and personality patterns, entirely different from what the generalized Euro-American psychological theories suggest (Trimble, 2000). These Western counselling and therapy modules do not fit to the need of people from another culture. Therefore, an effective

---

[2] The Diagnostic and Statistical Manual of Mental Disorders (DSM) is the standard classification of mental disorders used by mental health professionals in the United States. The Diagnostic and Statistical Manual of Mental Disorders, is now in its fifth edition DSM-5. Published by the American Psychiatric Association (APA), it offers a common language and standard criteria for the classification of mental disorders. Similarly, WHO has ICD, produced by a global health agency with a constitutional public health mission, unlike DSM which is produced by a single national professional association. ICD is not only global but also multidisciplinary and multilingual.

therapist should work in harmony with background influences of human condition specifically the tradition, life-world, environmental and geographic conditions of the clients. I am of the opinion that it is necessary that cross-cultural approach should be replaced by culture-specific approach in identifying human conditions, cliental problems and therapeutic interventions. It is here that phenomenology puts its leg strong. Therefore every therapist should be culturally competent.

We can make a difference between culture-specific psychology and cross-cultural psychology. Cross-cultural psychology views culture simply as a site of variations for human behaviour, whereas, culture-specific psychology considers culture as the birthplace for psychological processes, an essential tool not only in therapy but also in every understanding of human behaviour. Psychologists are becoming more and more aware of cultural relativism and focus increasingly on cultural contextualization in understanding and answering human behaviour and mental health issues (Cole, 1996).

Postmodern counsellors and psychotherapists identify the deficiency in cross-cultural counselling and they stress the need to understand human phenomena in relation to specific culture rather than accepting generalized universal truths (Yeo, 2000). Therefore, to be a competent therapist one should be open to the subjective cultural concepts, ethnic identities, and develop culture-specific approaches in order to understand the patients. As Bruner (1990) points out,

> "*Scientific psychology . . . will achieve a more effective stance toward the culture at large when it comes to recognize that the folk psychology of ordinary people is not just a set of self-assuaging illusions, but the culture's beliefs and working hypotheses about what makes it possible and fulfilling for people to live together. . . It is where psychology starts and wherein it is inseparable from anthropology . . .* " (p. 32).

This awareness and focus on culture-specific psychology makes phenomenology applicable in understanding and helping clients from different socio-cultural background in their specific culture. In short, culture-specific psychology opens vistas for 'less pre-conceptions, less hypothesizing, out of presupposition and assumptions', *therefore, a competent culture-specific therapist should be a phenomenologist.*

Phenomenological Counselling*:* Postmodern thinkers identify existential situatedness as a factor in which our being presents itself to awareness and the human individual and surrounding environment are intertwined. Human beings can't be isolated from history, culture and language. Due to this fact, phenomenology has become a clinical method that explores the quality of lived experiences (Frie, 2003). As Heidegger (1962) points out "to let that which shows itself be seen from itself in the very way in which it shows itself from itself" (p. 58).

From the traditional psychoanalysis to the present day transpersonal approach, we can see psychologists trying to apply phenomenology to both research and practice. For example, Freudian Psychoanalysis has phenomenological approach in its therapy. As Merleau-Ponty (1979) points out,

"It would be a mistake to imagine that even with Freud, psychoanalysis rules out the description of psychological motives, and is opposed to the phenomenological method; psychoanalysis has, on the contrary ... as Freud puts it, that every human action has a meaning" (p. 158).

In psychoanalysis the therapist by way of free associations gives attention to anything that comes to awareness. Here, psychoanalysis is very similar to the phenomenological method. However, we can establish some differences in psychoanalysis and phenomenological interpretation: in psychoanalysis all data are interpreted by its own theoretical assumptions, whereas phenomenological approach insists subjects interpreting their human condition from their own life-world.

The following two concepts from anthropology: *Etic* and *Emic* are very important in understanding culture-specific, cultural competent understanding of human condition. *Emic* approach seeks to understand reality (human experiences, feelings, emotions) from the view of its adherents, while the *etic* approach does the same but by means of analytical tools and concepts drawn from outside (Pelto & Pelto, 1978). An *etic* approach understands the phenomenon cross-culturally where as *emic* approach understands culture-specifically. Studying culture according to pre-established e*tic* procedures impedes the discovery of cultural diversity, whereas *emic* analysis broadens the view (Headland, Pike & Harris, 1990). Also, the *emic* approach focuses on studying socio-cultural phenomena from within a specific cultural context and understanding, as the people from within that culture understand it (Gudykunst, 1997). Two specific areas, namely, research and practice where phenomenology can be applied to human condition in counselling and psychotherapy.

Research: There is a misconception among many social science research scholars that scientific research means 'experimental research or quantitative research'. Many scholars have prejudice towards qualitative or descriptive methodology. As Heppner, Kivlighan, and Wampold (1992) point out, descriptive or qualitative research does not fit the "pure science myth" (p. 194) of the experimental research mongers who reduce research to quantitative numbers. However, many social scientists agree the fact that quantitative methods are not privileged over qualitative methods or experimental methods over naturalistic approaches (Braud & Anderson, 1998). Besides this, descriptive research allows researchers to understand many variables more fully and to develop more worthwhile and useful studies. Therefore, social science researchers are becoming aware of the important place that descriptive qualitative research holds in the process of understanding the situatedness of people and to work within a framework of description and discovery. Qualitative research designs, drawn from anthropological and other social science research methods, depend on the written or spoken words and/or observable behaviours as data sources (Bloland, 1992). Phenomenological approach fits well into descriptive qualitative research because it involves observation and description of variables as they are distributed throughout a population.

Phenomenological research differs from ethnographic research. Ethnographic research involves observation and description of phenomena within a specific setting (Wiersma, 1995). The purpose of ethnographic research is to observe and document what occurs in particular setting without manipulating variables or imposing structure. Ethnographic research is not concerned with providing contextual data. Therefore, the emphasis is on observation and description of what occurs without pre-conceived hypotheses. Such research may generate hypotheses throughout the data-collection process and/or focus observations around these hypotheses (Wiersma, 1995). Phenomena are observed and documented within a specific environmental context. Analyses may involve some quantification, such as proportions or percentages, but primarily rely upon qualitative descriptions of the phenomena of interest.

Phenomenological research is similar to ethnographic research, but goes further gaining the subjects' understandings of environments, involvements, and experiences. Thus, phenomenological researchers collect data by interviewing and asking the subjects how they experience specific phenomena. Bracketing, that is, the deferment of the researcher's personal prejudices and biases and horizontalization, that is, treating all data as if it were equally important, are the specific tools used (Heppner, Kivlighan & Wampold, 1992).

Practice: In every counselling and therapy session, when a therapist and client meet, a cross-cultural communication takes place regardless of the racial, educational or socio-economic similarities between the two parties (Owen, 1989). Rigid *etic* approach or perspective creates this cross-cultural communication. When the therapist allows the client to define the problem to the client's own satisfaction, cross-cultural outlook gives room for culture specific outlook and this phenomenological outlook was brought out by Carl Rogers (Rogers, 1951).

In dealing with healing and therapy Castillo (1997) identifies disease-centred and client-centred approach. A disease-centred approach focuses on the symptoms observed and then makes a diagnosis. A client-centred approach on the other hand, focuses on the patient's worldview, how the client defines the illness and what the patient believes to be the cause of the illness. Consequently, a client-centred approach focuses on culture-sensitive assessment.

Let me give you a therapy situation: Mr. X comes to with two specific symptoms as presenting problems. a) his deceased father appears in dreams; b) he is not able to sleep. For a disease-centred therapist, here is a client who is not able to sleep and the therapy should be focused on helping the client to sleep well. Here again, a specific subjective experience of Mr. X is not considered as a unique experience rather it is considered a common symptom of sleep disorder. However, in the phenomenological approach, it is not so. As Panos and Panos (2000) pinpoint, offering a culture-sensitive therapeutic assessment will consider: What are the dominant cultural values and belief systems of the client? How does the client describe his experience of seeing his deceased father? How does the client define sleeping problem? What are the client's beliefs about the cause of sleeplessness? It is here, the salient feature of phenomenology is applied in counselling and psychotherapy. Although all the therapy do make use of phenomenological approach in one way or another, humanistic-existential therapy and transpersonal therapies are highly popular phenomenology based therapies.

Based on the worldview, philosophy, people and their existence, humanistic-existential approaches deal with important life themes. These themes include living and dying, freedom, responsibility to self and others, finding meaning in life, and dealing with a sense of meaninglessness. More than other kinds of therapists, existential therapists examine consciousness, individuals' awareness of themselves and their ability to look beyond their immediate problems and daily events to problems of human existence. The first existential therapists were European psychiatrists trained in psychoanalysis who were dissatisfied with Freud's emphasis on biological drives and unconscious processes. Existential therapists help their clients confront and explore anxiety, loneliness, despair, fear of death, and the feeling that life is meaningless. There are few techniques specific to existential therapy. Therapists normally draw on techniques from a variety of therapies. A popular existential therapy is *logotherapy,* developed by Austrian psychiatrist Viktor E. Frankl in the 1940s.

Person-centred therapy, originally called client-centred therapy, is perhaps the best-known form of phenomenology-based therapy. American psychologist Carl Rogers developed it in the 1940s and 1950s. Carl Rogers believed that within each person, there lies a capacity for self-understanding and constructive change. Often, it is clouded by emotional struggles and goalless living. In *Rogerian* form of counselling and psychotherapy, people are helped toward growth, maturity, and life enrichment in their own perspective rather than the clinician's.

Transpersonal approach is an emerging trend in psychology. Transpersonal approach explicitly addresses the subjective human experiences. Thus transpersonal psychotherapy emerges above the medical model of remedial work and handles spiritual issues too. It can also be identified as a bridge between the eastern and western belief system integrated in psychotherapy.

The word transpersonal comes from two words: *trans* (beyond or through) and *persona* (mask or façade). At first transpersonal approach in psychology and psychotherapy became widely used to refer to any human experience related to religion, spirituality, meditation and mysticism (Daniels, 1998). However, today it covers a wider variety of subjective phenomena, not necessarily religious or spiritual. It is also a process of harmonious blending of subjective experiences in psychology which are often neglected by traditional, conventional therapeutic approaches. From the many definitions and views of transpersonal psychology, Lajoie & Shapiro (1992) identify the following five elements as the basic characteristics of transpersonal psychology. They are: (a) an interest in states of consciousness, (b) concern with human being's highest or ultimate potential, (c) human experience that goes beyond ego or personal self, (d) the idea of transcendence, and (e) a spiritual dimension in human life.

Abraham Maslow, the architect of humanistic psychology, is considered one of the pioneers of transpersonal psychology. The great importance Maslow gave to self-actualization, peak experiences etc as the highest attainable motivations and goals of humans, place him as the great explorer of the transpersonal in human beings (Walsh & Vaughan, 1993). In the theories of Carl Rogers, Fritz Perls and Viktor Frankl too, transpersonal ideas are seen although not identified purely as such.

A transpersonal approach sees human beings as intuitive, mystical, psychic and spiritual (Hendricks & Weinhold, 1982). Psychology considers development and the formation of a stable, integrated, and individuated ego as the goal of human development and mental health whereas transpersonal psychology exceeds such description of psychological theories and explores stages of personality development that extend beyond the individual ego into transpersonal realms (Wilber, 2000). However, it is important to distinguish bizarre phenomenon from transpersonal experience or phenomenon. Daniels (1998) argues that any event or experience or phenomenon that has a transformational meaning or effect on a person can be considered subject matter for transpersonal psychology. Therefore wide ranges of paranormal experiences are included in the subject matter of transpersonal psychology.

Today there is a great awareness among psychologists and postmodern thinkers to move from cross-cultural paradigm to culture-specific in understanding human condition. Phenomenology comes in as a qualitative research method as well as therapeutic modality to facilitate clients to make sense of their life-world. Thus, with the help of *emic* understanding, grounded in phenomenological approach, we can work on the therapist-client relationship in a better way, with a genuine understanding of client's life-world and thus, resolve wide varieties of therapeutic concerns.

Ten

Indian Psychology & Counselling

$\mathfrak{I}$ndian psychology as it is understood today is an antiquated blend of philosophy, theology, cosmology and mythology of ancient Indian civilization. This is similar to the Western psychology in the pre-Wundt era. Western psychology has its origin and linkage to the ancient Greek philosophy of Socrates, Plato and Aristotle and in the medieval period adjusted and modified by various other European philosophies and the Christian theology of Aquinas. By establishing the world's first experimental psychology laboratory at Leipzig, Wilhelm Wundt gave a scientific outlook to psychology in 1879 and liberated it from the clutches of religious assumptions and abstract philosophical speculations. The Russians too had their share with similar scientific endeavours highlighted by the experiments of Ivan Pavlov. These initiatives produced serious, systematic and radical changes in the scope, outlook and the nature of Western psychology which elevated the human behavioural study on par with other empirical sciences. Unfortunately this has not taken place to this point in the Indian subcontinent.

The problem with many scholars who exert their efforts in defining Indian Psychology today is that they magnify the ancient mystical, mythological and puranic cosmological thoughts and the assorted religio-philosophical systems as glorified psychological thinking rather than giving practical and pragmatic principles guiding to comprehensive theories of human behaviour in accordance with the emerging worldview in the changing society. Therefore, Indian psychology remains today as a primordial, intuitive and unscientific thought pattern of bundled subjective assumptions eluding concrete empirical investigation.

In this current backdrop, the practice of counselling and psychotherapy in India could be identified in the following way:

- Majority of the psychologists have only the background in Western psychology and related theories and therapy techniques
- They use therapy processed as they were taught and trained without realising any cross-cultural barriers
- A small minority, who do realise this handicaps in applying Western therapy modes are left with no clear alternative options and therefore integrate some Indian techniques in their own way and style
- There are also very few therapists who adhere to traditional Indian psychology which is based on classical religio-philosophical thoughts and try their own therapy models with little scientific stance and concern

Since there are no accurate therapy reports and research based evaluation of outcome, it is difficult to conclude what contributes to the best therapy outcome. However, it is the opinion of many scholars in the field of psychology and the vast majority of the therapists who practice Western models or those who minimally integrate local concepts, that there is an immediate need for culture-specific theories for better understanding of client's problems leading to the enhanced therapy outcome. In the case of therapists who use the traditional Indian psychology, the fixation and the associated obsession with the glorified supremacy of ancient Indian philosophy and the related knowledge base, they are blind to the fact that there is a need for culture-specific theories that could explain human phenomenon in a much better way as it is lived today.

The uniqueness of Indian socio-cultural context creates challenges to psychologists due to the questionable accuracy and applicability of Euro-American theories that are being used in various social science disciplines and psychological counselling in particular. How far cross-cultural theories have soundness for Indian application? How far are the Western theories unassailable for Indian cultural context? These are some of the exigent questions that highlight the need for indigenous theories.

One of the major constraints identified in doing quality therapy in the Indian context is lack of theories and principles to explain human behaviour in the current socio-cultural, politico-economic situation in India. This is followed by limitations in culture-sensitive counsellor and psychology education, resulting in lack of appropriate indigenous therapy models and techniques. The alternative suggested by some Indian scholars to this pressing need is the archaic Indian psychology which in turn does not reflect the current worldview of the people, lacks application to existing socio-cultural context and also empirical stance.

In the first place, a thorough study of current culture which would comprise the changing family life, urbanisation, globalised education, mass media, growing technology are necessary in the backdrop of traditional Indian culture. This will help one to identify the discrepancies in Western theories of human behaviour so that human behaviour in India could be understood accurately. These empirical principles and solid theories should replace both the Western theories as well as the current antiquated Indian psychology with contemporary understanding of human behaviour. These new scientific principles and theories should be taught in counsellor education that in turn will pave the way for indigenous counselling and psychotherapy.

Although the need for indigenizing knowledge base has been raised in various circles, there are not many notable initiatives taken in the grass root level to establish indigenous theories. If this is done, it would offer a wonderful basis for understanding human behaviour and socially responsive knowledge base as well as cultural sensitive psychology and therapy modalities.

Another obstacle identified in doing psychotherapy using Western therapy models in India, is the counselling structure and the process, when they are blindly applied to Indian clients. The following key specifications and differences are identified in the counselling structure and process[3].

a) *Duration of therapy*: Generally in the Western therapy models, one sessions last for around 50 minutes. In the Indian context it has been noted that the duration of a single session is often extended to 90 minutes. 50 minutes seems very short period.

b) *Family background*: In the initial phase of counselling, the therapist needs to know thoroughly the family background of the client in order to understand the presenting problem of the client and also to define the problem itself. Unlike the Western cultures in which the client's problems are easily understood by understanding the client's individual background, in the Indian setup almost all the cliental problems are one or other way family related. This is due to the close tie between family members, either joint or extended family system. Even if the couple form nuclear family, they are not completely free from family cobweb.

---

[3] This is the result of a longitudinal study by the researcher for over seven years, utilizing Autoethnography qualitative research method. This paper was presented in the 2nd Asia Pacific-Rim International Counselling Conference, Hong Kong 2011.

c) *Sharing personal experience and that of other clients in the therapy interventions:* One of the highly recommended and appreciated features in the process and therapy intervention is the counsellor sharing his own experience or that of another client who has similar problems and issues. This gives confidence in the client thinking that he or she is not the only person having this problem.

d) *Use of proverbs, sayings in the therapy interventions*: Greater importance is given by the clients when the counsellor uses proverbs and sayings of great men to stimulate change.

e) *Counsellor a self appointed expert*: Normally the clients expect a readymade answer for all their problems from a counsellor. Although the counsellor deals with the personal problems of the clients they expect the counsellor to give solutions to their problems. Precautions should be taken in this regard because if a counsellor emphatically contradicts such expectations of the client would lose the confidence of the client which in turn would affect therapy out come.

f) *Healing is an act of divine intervention*: A strong religious belief among the people even if they are not enthusiastically practising religion is that healing is an act of divine intervention and the role of therapist is being an agent of healing. In this regard the personal characteristics of the healer specifically the appearance and the attire take precedence over qualification. This is also noted that the apparent attraction for people to approach various bare-foot counsellors and religious heads for therapeutic assistance is their strong religious tones in exercising therapy. Among the clients surveyed more than 60 percent of the middle aged and elderly clients expect the therapist to use one of another reference to God and prayer in the therapy interventions. Among the younger generation nearly 35 percent expect the therapist to insert religious aspects in the therapy process.

g) *Termination of therapy*: In the Western models, termination of counselling is a step in which the counsellor needs to explain the client the progress and come to a contractual understanding of cessation. However in the Indian context termination is not a serious issue because once cured or relieved from the problem it is often understood that the client will not come for counselling even if the counsellor requests the client to appear for counselling. So it is often understood when a client does not appear for counselling, s/he is relieved of the issues or given up.

h) *Multicultural competence*: India is a country of various languages, religion, caste, customs and practices. There are cultural differences even among people of two different caste living in a same village or same caste living in two different villages. Counselling in this multicultural setting is a big challenge for any therapist. It is not enough to be Indian to do quality therapy, one need to know the cultural diversity of the people at various levels. Therefore India calls for every therapist to be a multicultural therapist, either working in rural or urban setting.

In the milieu of emerging trends in the Indian sub-continent for the growing need for therapeutic counselling and psychotherapy and the current difficulties and inconsistencies in doing quality therapy to enhance the mental wellbeing of people, indigenous therapy models are highly recommended. This following indigenous therapy model, not purely based on the ancient belief system that is popularly understood as Indian psychology, rather studying the contemporary socio-cultural life-world of the people and creating culture specific theories to explain the life that is lived and experienced today.

Indigenous Counselling: Based on various findings and the experiential knowledge, a phenomenological, transpersonal therapy model will suit the Indian population better than Western therapy or counselling models. Transpersonal approach is gaining popularity as an integrative therapy modality in which many disciplines merge together. It embraces an oriental worldview that incorporates elements of personal mysticism, native philosophy, cosmology and traditional culture and worldview. Thus transpersonal counselling and psychotherapy is very much in tune with Eastern cultures and worldview that goes in tune with meditation, yoga, shamanic and traditional healings, therapeutic touch, *reiki*, acupuncture, and other supernatural, mystical and psychic practices. Many cultural components could be very well integrated into psychotherapy and counselling, provided the counsellor or therapist is very intuitive, creative and skilled.

Taken into consideration the various inadequacies of the current therapy practice and the uniqueness of India psyche, the following six stage counselling model is prepared. This model uses both phenomenological elements in understanding the human experience in its situatedness as well as culture-specific understanding of personal experiences, family culture and worldview of the people.

In the first place, the counsellor/therapist must be aware and accept that people do have unique worldview emerging from their belief system both religio-philosophical and cultural leading to their unique health concepts. This together with another counsellor characteristic, that is, an unconditional approach in accepting the clients as they are together with their problems, but also accepting the client's problem in their belief system. This identification of problem from the point of client's worldview should be the basic philosophy of counselling. These counsellor characteristics, the philosophy of counselling and unconditional acceptance of client's belief system make the therapist a welcome person to open the problems of the client. In the Indian scenario, an elaborate family background of the client needs to be probed in order to understand the unique family dynamics of the client together with the belief system regarding the causes of sickness. Indians generally are family oriented people and the collective mind set as against individual living plays a vital role in therapy too, especially in identifying any problem both individual as well as social.

In the next stage, through that medium of respecting and accepting the personal experiences of the clients as they are and also identifying the client's specific concepts and views regarding healing, the therapy process should be directed. Sometimes this could be done together with the exploration of family background.

Once the belief system and the problems are explored together with the family dynamics of the client, the therapy process could be initiated. Help the client to re-establish a conscious relationship with self and others by different modalities applicable and acceptable to the individual. Some form of customary rituals and reconciliation (with self & others), if the client's problem demands, could be combined in the therapy process. Reconciliation, with the self, others or even spiritual and religious forces is a main factor that need to be adopted in the therapy process.

Meditation as such is an integral part of Indian psyche and that could be very well utilised in various means and modalities. The following are some explicit techniques that could be integrated into the therapy process: if the client relies on factors outside his or her self to facilitate healing ask the client to close the eyes and visualize them as a healing technique. If the client is religious, some acts of reconciliation with God, seeking forgiveness of God could be suggested. Prayer and meditation could be encouraged because many such practices of various religious sects are similar to catharsis; Indian meditation brings out the same effects of imagery and relaxation techniques. If the client has no religious beliefs, focus on some values and spirituality of the client (doing justice, possessing rationality and free will to decide, etc.).

The use of sayings from ancient wisdom, proverbs and words of eminent people would inspire the people for a quick realisation of problems.

In the final step, facilitate and help the client to build new patterns of thought, feeling and behaviour (based on the belief system either religious or spiritual) by way of meditation, visualization and autosuggestions. As the session comes to an end, a piece of therapeutic touch (in which the therapist touches the client in consolation or as a sign of blessing) which is one of the earliest and widely seen healing practises all over the world and traditions could be employed. This can create wide range of positive impacts in the client. If the client is very religious, a word of promise 'I will pray for you...' will bring enormous amount of positive feelings and confidence that can generate extra-boost to the healing process.

Psychology evolved purely as a scientific endeavour in 1879 by Wilhelm Wundt and strengthened by behaviourists J B. Watson, B. F. Skinner, etc., is a strong force today in defining human behaviour and psychotherapy. In India such initiatives have not yet been started, although the country has great traditional indigenous knowledge base. There is a strong need for local theories to explain the current life situation, human behaviour and above all the need for an indigenous culture-specific psychotherapy. As modern cultures and technologies spread around the world, the traditional cultural practices diminish continually as older generations pass away and younger generations slowly set aside their traditional ways and adapt to new life styles. However, the psyche still holds on the remnants of the past and, traditions. Sometimes it can create or lead to inner conflicts too. Therefore many researchers are now placing a greater emphasis on recording indigenous cultures and knowledge.

A therapist who recognizes the cultural practices, belief system and health concepts behind the client's illness and healing can do therapy in a very comfortable way. Indian traditional Psychology based on religio-philosophical concepts need to be incorporated into theories of human behaviour and daily living, so that current life and behaviour of the people could be explained precisely and perfectly for a better therapy outcome.

References

1. Adair, J. G., Puhan, B. N., & Vohra, N. (1993). Indigenization of psychology: Empirical assessment of progress in Indian research. International Journal of Psychology, 28, 149-169.
2. Benor, D. J. (1999). Holistic Integrative Care. Retrieved October 20, 2009 from http://www.wholistichealingresearch.com
3. Bloland, P. A. (1992). Qualitative research in student affairs. Los Angeles, CA: University of California at Los Angeles.
4. Braud. W. & Anderson. R. (1998). Transpersonal research methods for the social sciences. New Delhi: Sage Publications.
5. Bruner, J. (1990). Acts of meaning. Cambridge: Harvard University Press.
6. Castillo, R. J. (1997). Cultural assessment. "In" R. J. Castillo, Culture and mental illness (pp. 55-75). Pacific Grove, CA: Brooks/Cole.
7. Chatterjee, S., Chowdhary, N., Pednekar, S., Cohen, A., Andrew, G, Araya, R., Simon, G. (2008). Integrating evidence-based treatments for common mental disorders in routine primary care: Feasibility and acceptability of the MANAS intervention in Goa. World Psychiatry 7, 39-46.
8. Clay, R. A. (2002). An indigenized psychology: Psychologists in India blend Indian traditions and Western psychology. Monitor on Psychology. Vol 33, No. 5.
9. Cole, M. (1996). Cultural psychology: A once and future discipline. Cambridge, MA: Harvard University Press.

10. Daniels, M. (1998). Transpersonal psychology and the paranormal. Transpersonal Psychology Review, 2(3), 17-31.

11. Edman, J. L. & Kameoka, V. A. (1997). Cultural differences in illness schemas: An analysis of Filipino and American ill attributions. Journal of Cross-Cultural Psychology, 28(3), 252-266.

12. Frie, R. (2003). (Ed.) Understanding experience. NY: Routledge.

13. Funk, K. (2001). What is a worldview? Retrieved March 28, 2010 from http://www.engr.orst.edu/~funkk

14. Ganguli, H. C. (2000). Epidemiological findings on prevalence of mental disorders in India. Indian Journal of Psychiatry 42, (1): 14-20.

15. Gorden, R. L. (1969). Interviewing: Strategy, Techniques and Tactics Homewood Ill, Dorsey Press.

16. Gudykunst, W. B. (1997). Cultural variability in communication. Communication Research, 24 (4): 327-348.

17. Headland, T. N. Pike K. L., & Harris M. (1990). (Ed.). "Emics" and "Etics": The insider/outsider debate. London: Sage Publications.

18. Heidegger, M. (1962). Being and time. Oxford, Basil Blackwell.

19. Hendricks, G., & Weinhold, B. (1982). Transpersonal approaches to counseling and psychotherapy. London: Love Publishing Company.

20. Heppner, P. P., Kivlighan, D. M., & Wampold, B. E. (1992). Research design in counselling. Pacific Grove, CA: Brooks/Cole.

21. Hultkrantz, A. (1992). Shamanic healing and ritual drama. New York: Crossroad.

22. Husserl, E. (1970). Logical investigations New York, Humanities Press.

23. Jacob, K. S., Sharan, P., Mirza, I., Garrido-Cumbrera, M., Seedat, S. Mari, J. J., Sreenivas, V. & Saxena, S. (2007). Mental health systems in countries: Where are we now? The Lancet 370, (September 22).

24. Jain, A. K., (2005). Psychology in India, *The Psychologist*, Vol 18 No 4.

25. Janetius, S.T. (2003). Emerging worldview of Cordillera Indigenous people in the Philippines: Implications for Psychotherapy. Un-published Doctoral Dissertation, De La Salle University, Manila.

26. Janetius, S. T., Mini T. C. & Ravishankar, D. (2009). Sex taboos and the emerging worldview of rural Indian society, Paper presented in the 8th Biennial Conference of the Asian Association of Social Psychology, Indian Institute of Technology, Delhi, December 11-14, 2009.

27. Janetius, S. T., Mini T. C. & Alemayehu, T. (2010). Abyssinia in the new millennium: culture and higher education in Ethiopia, Thrissur: Mishil & Js Publishers.

28. Kearney, R. (1984). Dialogues with contemporary continental thinkers. Manchester: Manchester University Press.

29. Kennedy, M. (2010). India's Mentally Ill Turn To Faith, Not Medicine, International Reporting Project, www.internationalreportingproject.org/stories/detail/1588

30. Krippner, S. (1988). Shamans: The first healers. In G. Doore (Ed.), Shaman's path: Healing, personal growth and empowerment (pp. 101-114). Boston, MA: Shambala Publications.

31. Lajoie, D. H., & Shapiro, S. I. (1992). Definitions of transpersonal psychology: The first twenty-three years. Journal of Transpersonal Psychology, 24(1), 79-98.Leith, M. (2003). The three worldviews framework. Retrieved January 13, 2009 from www.martinleith.com

32. Leith, M. (2003). The three worldviews framework. Retrieved January 13, 2009 from http://www.martinleith.com/worldviews/welcome.html

33. Measor, L. (1985). Interviewing: a Strategy in Qualitative Research in R Burgess (ed) Strategies of Educational Research: Qualitative Methods. Lewes: Falmer Press.

34. Merleau-Ponty, M. (1979). Phenomenology of perception. N.J.: The Humanities Press.

35. Mills. J. (1999). In search of a method: New directions in philosophical counselling. Paper presented at Canadian Society for Philosophical Practice, Ontario Philosophical Association, Guelph.

36. National family health survey, India, 2005-2006: Tamil Nadu.

37. Oakley, A. (1981). "Interviewing women: a contradiction in terms" in H. Roberts (ed) Doing Feminist Research .London

38. Offiong, D. (1999). Traditional healers in the Nigerian health care delivery system and the debate over integrating traditional and scientific medicine. Anthropological Quarterly, 72(3), 118-131.

39. Owen, R. I. (1989). The application of some ideas from anthropology to counselling, therapy and cross-cultural counselling. British Association for Counselling and the American Association for Counselling Development.: Uxbridge University.

40. Panos, P. T., & Panos, A. J. (2000). A model for a culture-sensitive assessment of patients in health care settings.Social Work in Health Care, 31(1), 49-62.

41. Pelto, P. J., & Pelto. G. H. (1978). Units of observation: "Emic" and "Etic" approaches. "In" Anthropological research: The structure of inquiry. Cambridge: Cambridge University Press.

42. Plummer, K. (1983). Documents of Life: an introduction to the problems and literature of a humanistic method. London, Unwin Hyman.

43. Rajamohan, G. (2004). Higher reaches of Indian psychology. Retrieved December 10, 2010 from www.lifepositive.com

44. Ramakrishna, J. & Weisss, M.G. (1992). Health, illness, and immigration: East Indians in the United States. The Western Journal of Medicine, 157(3), 265-271.

45. Rogers, C.R. (1951). Client-centred therapy. Boston: Houghton

46. Santos, D. (1998). Multicultural perspective in three international schools in the Philippines. In Bernado, (Ed.),Understanding behavior bridging cultures (pp 159 – 166). Manila: De La Salle University Press.

47. Sinha, D. (1994). Origins and development of psychology in India: Outgrowing the alien framework. *International Journal of Psychology, 29*(6), 695-705.

48. Sinha, D. (1997). Indigenising psychology. In J. W. Berry, Y. H. Poortinga, & J. Pandey (Eds.), *Handbook of Cross-cultural Psychology*, Vol 1. (pp.129-169). Needham Heights, MA: Allyn & Bacon.

49. Sinha, J.B.P. (1993). The bulk and the front of psychology in India. Psychology and Developing Societies, 5(2), 135-150.

50. Sinha, J.B.P. (2000). Towards indigenization of psychology in India. Psychological Studies, 45(1&2), 3-13.

51. Soundararajan, R., (2009). Relevance of indigenous models of counseling in Indian context, Indian Journal of Social Science Researches, Vol. 6, No. 2, pp. 133-136.

52. Spiegelberg, H. (1970). Phenomenology, in Encyclopaedia Britannica, vol. 17 (14th ed), pp. 810-812.

53. Thara, R. & Srinivasan, T.N. (2000). How stigmatizing is schizophrenia in India. Indian Journal of Psychiatry, 46, 235 - 241.

54. Trimble, J. E. (2000). Considering the cultures within. Retrieved October 14, 2001 from http://www.radcliffe.edu/quarterly

55. Vontress, C. (2009). Traditional healing Holistic intervention. Retrieved on April 12, 2010 from http://www.oise.utoronto.ca

56. Walsh, R., & Vaughan, F. (1993). Paths beyond ego: The transpersonal vision. LA: Tarcher-Putnam.

57. Weil, A. (1995). Spontaneous healing. New York: Knopf.

58. WHO (2005). Mental health atlas 2005. World Health Organization: 232-5.

59. Wiersma, W. (1995). Research methods in education (6th ed.). Boston, MA: Allyn and Bacon.

60. Wilber, K. (2000). Sex, ecology, spirituality: The spirit of evolution (2nd rev. ed.). Boston: Shambhala.

61. Yeo, A. (2000). Counseling trends in postmodernist thinking in counseling. "In" Clemeña (Ed.), Counseling in Asia (pp. 6-19). Manila: De La Salle University Press.

Author Index

Adair, J. G. 20
Alemayehu, T. 18
Anderson, R. 80
Andrew, A. 9
Aquinas, Thomas. 91
Araya, R. 9
Aristotle. 91
Benor, D.J. 19, 57
Binswanger, 74
Bloland, P. A. 81
Boss, 74
Braud, W. 80
Bruner,J. 78
Castillo, R.J. 82
Charles Tart. 68
Chatterjee. 9
Chowdhary, N. 9
Clay, R. A. 11
Cohen, A. 9
Cole, M. 77
Daniels, M. 85, 86
Edman, J. L. 19
Freud, S. 25, 28, 29, 79, 84
Frie, R. 26, 78
Funk, K. 17
Ganguli, H. C. 8
Garrido-Cumbrera. 8
Gorden, R. L. 74
Gudykunst, W. B. 80
Harris, M. 80
Headland, T. N. 80
Heidegger, M. 74, 78
Hendricks, G. 86

Heppner, P. P. 80, 82
Hultkrantz, A. 4
Husserl, E. 73, 74
Jacob, K. S. 8
Jain, A. K., 11
Janetius, 3, 7 ,8, 17, 18, 76
Jaspers. 74
Jung, Carl. 68
Kameoka, V.A. 19
Kearney, R. 74
Kennedy, M. 6
Kivlighan, D. M. 80, 82
Krippner. 25
Lajoie, D. H. 83
Leith, M. 17
Mari,J.J. 8
Maslow, A. 68, 85
Measor, L. 74
Merleau-Ponty, M. 79
Mills, J. 74
Mini, T. C. 7, 8, 18
Mirza, I. 8
Oakley, A. 74
Offiong, D. 18
Owen, R. I. 82
Panos, A.J. 83
Panos, P. T. 83
Pavlov, Ivan. 91
Pednekar, S. 9
Pelto, G. H. 79
Pelto, P.J. 79
Perls, Fritz. 86
Pike, K. L. 80

Plato. 91
Plummer, K. 74
Puhan, B. N. 20
Ramakrishna, J. 18
Ravishankar, D. 7, 8
Roberts, Jane. 68
Rogers, Carl. 82, 84, 86
Santos, D. 76
Saxena, S. 8
Seedat, S. 8
Shapiro, S. I. 85
Sharan, P. 8
Simon, G. 9
Sinha, D. 10
Sinha, J. B. P. 20
Skinner, B.F. 68, 102
Socrates. 91
Soundararajan, R. 11
Spiegelberg, H. 73
Sreenivas, V. 8
Srinivasan, T. N. 5
Stanislav Grof, 68

Thara, R. 5
Trimble, J. E. 20,76
Vaughan, F. 86
Viktor E. Frankl. 84, 86
Vohra, N. 20
Vontress, C. 4
Walsh, R. 86
Wampold, B. E. 80,82
Watson, J. B. 68, 102
Weil, A. 4
Weinhold, B. 86
Weisss, M .G. 18
Wiersma, W. 81
Wilber, Ken, 68, 86
Wundt, W. 10, 68, 91, 102
Yeo, A. 77

About the Author

Dr Janetius has established himself as a Cultural Psychologist with his vast experience in the Philippines, Ethiopia, Australia and India that spans over two decades. He earned his doctorate in Psychology with a German Scholarship from the reputed De La Salle University, Philippines, studying the 'Emerging worldview and healing practices of Indigenous Cordillera People in the Philippines' and classified their sickness as Pneumasomatic, a term used for the very first time in his Dissertation. His continuous research has produced numerous unique indigenous, culture-specific models and concepts in the fields of psychology, counselling, and education. Currently, he is the Director of Centre for Counselling and Guidance in an autonomous college in India.

Notes

Notes

www.ingramcontent.com/pod-product-compliance
Lightning Source LLC
Chambersburg PA
CBHW050456290526
45786CB00006B/2323